PRAISE FOR THE SERIES

In three short books, Pastor Joe Thorn offers a helpful treatment on the local church that is biblical, baptistic, and Calvinistic—and simultaneously fresh and practical. This is ideal for those who desire a better understanding of what the church is designed to be and do as a community of faith seeking to follow Jesus into the world with the gospel.

In *The Heart of the Church*, Thorn walks the reader through the gospel and related doctrines, demonstrating how what we believe forms who we are as God's people. In *The Character of the Church*, the essential components of a church are laid out in a clear and practical way, showing what is needed for overall church health. In *The Life of the Church*, Thorn offers a fresh perspective on how the church can live on mission for the glory of God and the good of others in tangible ways.

ED STETZER
Billy Graham Distinguished Chair, Wheaton College

————

I'd like to pass out *The Character of the Church* to every one of our church members. It's that good! It's a simple yet profound primer on the nature of the church. It gives a brief overview on the authority of the Bible, the ordinances, matters of church membership, and church discipline. These are essential for all believers to know and understand.

DAVE FURMAN
Pastor, Redeemer Church of Dubai, and author of *Being There: How to Love Those Who Are Hurting*

The Life of the Church is a helpful treatise on worship that will edify the church. Joe is careful to ensure his exhortations spring from Scripture itself, which makes this book applicable for Christians everywhere. It was a joy to read about the many aspects of the life that Christ has purchased for us with His own blood.

GLORIA FURMAN
Cross-cultural worker and author of *Missional Motherhood* and *Alive in Him*

The Heart of the Church is a brief and accessible theology of the gospel. It is simple, but not simplistic. It offers profound truths in everyday language. This book will help new Christians and serve as an encouraging reminder to mature ones.

RICHARD C. BARCELLOS
Pastor, Grace Reformed Baptist Church in Palmdale, CA, and author of *The Lord's Supper as a Means of Grace*

THE

heart

OF THE

CHURCH

—

THE GOSPEL'S HISTORY,
MESSAGE, AND MEANING

—

JOE THORN

MOODY PUBLISHERS
CHICAGO

Scripture quotations are from the ESV® Bible (The Holy Bible, English Standard Version®), copyright © 2001 by Crossway, a publishing ministry of Good News Publishers. Used by permission. All rights reserved.

Edited by Kevin P. Emmert
Cover and Interior Design: Erik M. Peterson
Author photo: Anthony Benedetto

ISBN: 978-0-8024-1470-0

Moody Publishers
820 N. LaSalle Boulevard
Chicago, IL 60610

1 3 5 7 9 10 8 6 4 2

Printed in the United States of America

To my brothers and sisters in the Acts 29 Network and
the Southern Baptist Convention, who preach
the gospel of Jesus Christ to the whole creation that the
heart of the church might spread across the earth.

contents

INTRODUCTION

The church today has a heart condition. She has not taken care of herself. As a result, she is sick. Modern religious doctors have written prescriptions to treat her lethargy, joylessness, fruitlessness, and weakening faith. But they are addressing only the symptoms, never getting to the root problem. The heart problem plaguing the modern church cannot be healed with new programs or innovative marketing tactics.

The root problem for many local churches is that the gospel no longer fills their hearts. We have been captivated by issues of secondary importance and have slowly drifted from our first love (Rev. 2:4). Many churches have let one particular issue, rather than the whole gospel, characterize the whole of their ministry. These issue-driven churches can be either conservative or liberal and can be found in every denomination. They may get the gospel right on paper but are animated and directed by other principles.

For example, some churches are driven by numbers. They want to see as many people as possible trust in Christ. No doubt, this desire is good, for God wants none to perish (2 Peter 3:9). But when we focus on numbers more than the gospel itself, we embrace pragmatism that encourages us to adopt any method that results in more people coming through the front doors of the church. This often leads to a weakening of both preaching and theology.

Some churches are driven by a desire to be culturally relevant, while other churches are focused on remaining culturally distinct. In both cases, something other than the cross is capturing the attention of the congregation. Some churches are driven by social or spiritual works that, while good, begin to eclipse the reason for all good works—the glory of God.

Some churches are driven by doctrinal purity. In the pursuit of the truth and love of theology, these churches become defined more by their theological heritage than by the Founder and Perfecter of our faith.

These issues are important in the life of a church, to be sure. But when they become what drive a church, the gospel loses its influence. When we are issue-driven, we end up being gospel-lite.

THE CENTRALITY OF THE GOSPEL

So what exactly is the gospel? In the simplest of terms, the gospel is the life, death, and resurrection of Jesus, all of which accomplishes redemption and restoration for all who believe in Him (1 Cor. 15:3–4; Col. 1:14; Heb. 9:11–12). In His life, Jesus fulfilled the law and accomplished all righteousness on behalf of sinners who have broken God's law at every point. In His death, Jesus atoned for our sins, satisfying the wrath of God and obtaining forgiveness for all who believe. In His resurrection, Jesus conquered sin and death, and guaranteed our victory over the same in and through Him. I will explain all this in greater detail throughout this book. But first, let us ask: given this basic definition of the gospel, what does gospel centrality look like?

To be gospel-centered means that the gospel, and ultimately Jesus Himself, is our greatest hope and boast, our deepest longing and joy, and our most passionate song and message. It means that the gospel is what defines us as Christians, unites us as brothers and sisters, changes us as sinners/saints and sends us as God's people into the world on mission. When we are gospel-centered, the gospel is exalted above every other good thing in our lives and triumphs over every bad thing set against us.

Gospel-centered churches do not ignore the issues that drive other churches, but they are not governed by them. Gospel-centered churches are driven by a love for Jesus and His work on our behalf. They are so focused on Jesus and the hope of redemption that they are passionate and articulate about their theology. Their desire to know and make Jesus known demands doctrinal precision and leads them to work toward seeing as many people as possible repenting of sin and trusting in Christ. When the gospel is central in a church, the church goes out into the world on mission while preserving its countercultural character as the people of God. The gospel-centered church is driven by love—for God and others—which leads to joyful obedience that points back to God.

In this first of three books exploring the heart, character, and life of the local church, I want to start with the gospel. I hope the following will encourage you and your church to prize above everything else the good news of Jesus Christ.

PART 1

the HISTORY OF THE GOSPEL

The gospel of Jesus Christ is not a mere set of propositions. It is not a lifestyle or a perspective on life. The gospel is not something we do. The gospel is historical truth. The gospel is something that happened—something God did for us.

To say it simply, the gospel is the life, death, and resurrection of Jesus. The apostle Paul expresses it this way:

> *For I delivered to you as of first importance what I also received: that Christ died for our sins in accor-*

*dance with the Scriptures, that he was buried, that
he was raised on the third day in accordance with
the Scriptures, and that he appeared to Cephas,
then to the twelve.*

(1 COR. 15:3–5)

The faith Paul embraced was grounded in three events: Jesus' righteous life, His atoning death, and His victorious resurrection from the grave. What we believe as Christians is not a philosophy, but a history. Even The Apostles' Creed, the oldest articulation of the faith following the apostolic era, demonstrates the historic nature of the Christian faith and even emphasizes the specific time period in which these events took place:

I believe in God the Father, Almighty, Maker of heaven
  and earth:
And in Jesus Christ, his only begotten Son, our Lord:
*Who was conceived by the Holy Ghost, born of the Virgin
  Mary:*
*Suffered under Pontius Pilate; was crucified, dead and
  buried: He descended into hell:*
The third day he rose again from the dead:
He ascended into heaven, and sits at the right hand of
  God the Father Almighty:
From thence he shall come to judge the quick and the
  dead:

I believe in the Holy Ghost:
I believe in the holy catholic church: the communion
 of saints:
The forgiveness of sins:
The resurrection of the body:
And the life everlasting. Amen.[1]

The gospel happened, and by it we are saved.

To say that the gospel is history is true, but that history has to be explained. What did Jesus accomplish by His life, death, and resurrection, and what does the believer receive from Him on account of these events? To interpret the history is the work of theology, and to do this we must rely on Scripture alone.

—

Chapter 1

THE THEME OF SCRIPTURE

The Bible is the Word of God. It is not merely great literature or a collection of inspiring religious stories. Scripture is the breathed-out Word of God that reveals His character, work, and will, as well as our nature, corruption, and redemption (see 2 Tim. 3:16). The whole Bible, all sixty-six books and letters, written by over forty authors over a span of approximately 1,400 years, is a unified and inspired whole that declares who God is, who we are, and what the purpose of creation is. Scripture is a perfect revelation, meaning that what it reveals is absolutely true, though not exhaustive. We cannot know everything about God, who is infinite, but He has revealed what we need to know about Him.

Unfortunately, it is not just the world that often misunderstands what the Bible really is. Christians too often hold wrong ideas of the Bible's nature, purpose, and usefulness. For instance, many believe the Bible is a kind of moral dictionary that answers every conceivable cultural question with perfect clarity. Others see the Bible as the roadmap to a fruitful spiritual life. Many churches today teach that the Bible is fundamentally about us and they promote the idea that in the sacred pages of Scripture are stories and truths designed to show us how we can be the heroes of our own lives. The Bible does reveal moral truth, spur spiritual growth, and includes us as participants in the story, but it is more than a moral dictionary. And it is not really about us.

The Bible, in all its parts, is one unified story of God's love for and salvation of sinners through His Son. From the opening pages of Genesis to the conclusion of Revelation, we discover the unfolding plan of God's work to redeem a people for His own possession through the life, death, and resurrection of Jesus Christ. He is the hero of Scripture, the full revelation of God, and the one to whom all Scripture points. Jesus is, as theologian Joel Beeke puts it, "the supreme focus, prism, and goal of God's revelation."[1]

CREATION AND COVENANT

The Bible begins with the creation of humanity as people made in God's image and for fellowship with Him. Bearing the image of God means that, in some ways, we look like God. Our innate sense of right and wrong, our capacity to rule well, to love, and to create—those are just a few of the ways we reflect God.

Not only that, we were made to live in communion with Him. We were created to love God and all His ways, to worship and obey Him. We were designed to have a relationship grounded in a covenant with God.

Covenants not only mark the movement of the history of redemption, but have always been the context for our relationship with God. What exactly is a covenant? In his book *The Covenant of Works: Its Confessional and Scriptural Basis*, pastor and author Richard Barcellos explains,

> A divine covenant with man may be very briefly defined as a divinely sanctioned commitment or relationship. In this sense, covenants come from God to man. They are not contracts between equal business partners. They are not up for negotiation.[2]

In the first chapters of Genesis, we learn that God created man and immediately established a covenant between Himself and us. He placed Adam and Eve in the garden and called them to be fruitful and to multiply, to maintain the garden, and to rule righteously over the world they inhabited. The one explicit prohibition given to Adam and Eve was not to eat from the Tree of Knowledge of Good and Evil. He gave them a warning, saying, "For in the day that you eat of it you shall surely die" (Gen. 2:15–17). Obedience would yield blessing and life (Gen. 2:9; 3:22); disobedience would yield punishment and death.

This covenant God made with Adam applied not only to him, but also to all humanity, as he was our first parent and our representative. Adam represented all humanity and was responsible for all humanity (Rom. 5:12–14). This was the beginning. It was marked by innocence and righteousness. But things did not remain this way for long.

THE SIN OF MAN

We do not know how long paradise lasted, but three chapters into the first book of the Bible, something catastrophic happens. Satan enters that perfect place and tempts Eve, the first woman, to disobey her God by eating of the Tree of Knowledge of Good and Evil. Satan, masquerading as a serpent, assured Eve that not only would she live, but that in eating of that tree she would also become like God.

Eve caved and ate the forbidden fruit, and Adam quickly followed. In that first act of treason, the first humans did not simply break a rule; they rejected the will of God and His place of supremacy in their lives. The covenant was broken.

This first sin not only disrupted fellowship between

God and our first parents. It opened a fissure between God and all of humanity, destroying our communion with Him. People originally created to be children of God became children of God's wrath (Eph. 2:1–3). Instead of resting in God's love, they fell into His judgment. In Adam, our representative, we all sinned and therefore became guilty of his transgression (Rom. 5:12).

From this point on in Scripture, the story is not only of man's sin, but of God's patience with and love for sinners. We broke our covenant with Him in the garden, but God held out another covenant though which sinners could be saved.

THE PROMISE OF SALVATION

Sin and judgment came quickly into the world, but the promise of deliverance came even quicker. The first "good news" sinners ever heard was offered to Adam and Eve just after their rebellion. We find it in the middle of God's judgment on their actions.

God cursed Adam, telling him that as a result of his disobedience, work would be marked by pain and toil (Gen. 3:17–18). Not only that, he would return to the ground from where he was taken (Gen. 3:19). In short, the world would never be the same for Adam in his vocation, recreation, and relationships.

Then God cursed Eve, telling her that the pain of

childbearing would be multiplied and that her "desire shall be contrary to your husband, but he shall rule over you" (Gen. 3:16). Eve, too, saw that not only was her relationship with God now broken, but so was her relationship with her husband and the rest of creation.

So far, the picture looks grim. But as God curses the Serpent, we find mercy and hope:

> *Because you have done this,*
>   *cursed are you above all livestock*
>   *and above all beasts of the field;*
> *on your belly you shall go,*
>   *and dust you shall eat*
>   *all the days of your life.*
> *I will put enmity between you and the woman,*
>   *and between your offspring and her offspring;*
> *he shall bruise your head,*
>   *and you shall bruise his heel.*

(GEN. 3:14–15)

As result of God's judgment on sin and evil, the anatomy of all serpents is changed. The devil, too, is cursed and is told that his destruction is coming. In that curse, God announces the remedy for our sinful condition: the offspring of the woman who will crush the serpent's head. This promise is not about humans battling snakes. Rather, it is a foretelling that a descendent of Eve will conquer the devil and put to end his work. This is the first preaching of the gospel, the good news that God will bring about salvation to the world through a Deliverer.

Despite God's promise of salvation, the world continued in sin and rebellion until Noah, who the Bible describes as a righteous man. After numerous generations continued to reject God, His patience finally came to an end. He told Noah that judgment would come upon the earth in the form of a flood. It would be catastrophic, and everyone would perish—except Noah and his family. God commanded Noah to build an ark, a large ship, so he and his family, along with a selection of the animals of the earth, would be saved.

The ark was built, the flood came, and the earth was covered in water. Noah and his family were spared, and after this divine act of justice, God established another covenant. He promised to never again destroy the earth with water, and He set the rainbow in the sky as a sign of His covenant to preserve creation (Gen. 9:9–17). This covenant would not save humans, but rather assured that God would preserve humanity and, in due time, save us through the offspring of Eve.

Centuries later, God established another covenant, this time with a man named Abram. God called Abram out of his homeland to make him a man of faith and the father of a great nation, one through whom the Savior would come. He changed Abram's name to Abraham, meaning "the father of many." God's promise guaranteed that Abraham and his wife, even in their old age, would conceive and bear a son, something they had been unable to do. This would be the beginning of the building of a nation. And through this nation, the whole world would be blessed (see Gen. 12; 15; 17).

Through Abraham and his descendants—Isaac, Jacob, and then Joseph—God created the nation of Israel. Israel was a people set apart by God to be His light in a dark world and through whom salvation would ultimately come, even to those outside of the nation. As the descendants of Abraham continued to increase, the Lord would formally establish the nation through a man named Moses. God used Moses to deliver His people from slavery in Egypt. Once free from Egypt's tyranny, God established yet another covenant.

Whereas the previous covenants were made with all humanity, this covenant was made exclusively with the nation of Israel. Like the covenant in the garden at the beginning, it included a promise of blessing if they obeyed God, but curses if they rebelled. The difference was that in this covenant—which we now call the "old covenant" or the Mosaic covenant—grace was also promised.

God gave the nation laws to obey that governed their

religious, civil, and social life. Israel was given a means by which justice and mercy could thrive among the people as they lived according to God's laws. The laws regarding worship, including priests (leaders in worship who mediated between God and the nation), a tabernacle (the place of worship), and the sacrifices (the depiction of God's wrath against sin taken away from His people and poured out on a substitute) not only gave structure to Israel's life of faith, but also pointed to the coming Deliverer who would be the perfect Priest, the blameless Sacrifice, and the one in whom all God's people would be gathered together.

Yet, this covenant itself could not give life to the people. It only revealed how corrupt the human heart had become, and that if justice and mercy were to be experienced in this world, it could not come by obedience to the law. The old covenant reinforced the need for redemption and deliverance through sacrifice. Yet their sacrifices were not what would ultimately bring salvation.

Israel experienced many ups and downs while living under the old covenant. When the people obeyed the Lord, the nation was blessed and was at peace. But when they continued in sin and committed idolatry, they came under God's judgment. In the midst of this cycle, God established another covenant, this time with a king.

King David was the ruler of Israel. He was a righteous king, a "man after God's heart," and God promised to bring a new and better King from David's line, who would rule in perfect righteousness and whose kingdom would have no end. The reign of this coming King would be far different than what Israel had come to experience. The reign of a mortal king lasted only so long. Even good kings were marred by sin and often brought trouble upon the nation. God's promise to David builds upon the promise that was made to Adam and Eve. One was coming who would reign in righteousness. God said to David,

> When your days are fulfilled and you lie down with
> your fathers, I will raise up your offspring after you,
> who shall come from your body, and I will establish
> his kingdom. He shall build a house for my name,
> and I will establish the throne of his kingdom
> forever.
>
> (2 SAM. 7:12–13)

God's original promise to Eve was repeated and clarified throughout the history of God's people, repeating the same promise of deliverance through a special Deliverer. In the Davidic covenant we learn that the victorious offspring of Eve would be a king.

The Lord also raised up prophets to speak to His people. These were men who would speak on behalf of God, warning of coming judgment for sin, while encouraging faith and repentance for the blessing of God. They often pointed to the future when the coming Savior would finally rescue and redeem the people from their enemies and their sin.

One of the most well-known prophecies concerning the coming Savior comes from the prophet Isaiah.

> *Who has believed what he has heard from us?*
>   *And to whom has the arm of the LORD been*
>   *revealed?*
> *For he grew up before him like a young plant,*
>   *and like a root out of dry ground;*
> *he had no form or majesty that we should look*
>   *at him,*
>   *and no beauty that we should desire him.*
> *He was despised and rejected by men,*
>   *a man of sorrows and acquainted with grief;*
> *and as one from whom men hide their faces*
>   *he was despised, and we esteemed him not.*
>
> *Surely he has borne our griefs*
>   *and carried our sorrows;*
> *yet we esteemed him stricken,*
>   *smitten by God, and afflicted.*
> *But he was pierced for our transgressions;*
>   *he was crushed for our iniquities;*
> *upon him was the chastisement that brought us*
>   *peace,*

and with his wounds we are healed.
All we like sheep have gone astray;
  we have turned—every one—to his own way;
and the LORD has laid on him
  the iniquity of us all.

(ISA. 53:1–6)

The picture of the Savior becomes clearer with this prophecy. While He would be a King, He would be one of the people and appear to be no one special. He would be rejected by His own people and crushed for sins He did not commit. He would be the sacrifice that saves others, and He would make sinners righteous.

The whole of the Old Testament is leading us to see Jesus with increasing clarity until He stands before us in the pages of the New Testament.

THE ARRIVAL OF SALVATION

The New Testament begins with the birth of Jesus Christ, the one to whom all these other biblical stories point. Jesus Himself reinforced this: "You search the Scriptures because you think that in them you have eternal life; and it is they that bear witness about me" (John 5:39). After reading from the book of Isaiah in the synagogue, He said, "Today this Scripture has been fulfilled in your hearing" (Luke 4:21). And as He walked with some of His disciples after His death and resurrection, He told them, "And beginning with Moses and all the Prophets, he interpreted to them in all the Scriptures the things concerning himself" (Luke 24:27).

Jesus, the Son of God, came to take away sin, fulfill all righteousness, establish a kingdom, and conquer the devil. He did it all through His life, death, and resurrection, which became the basis for God's final covenant—the new covenant.

In this covenant, perfect obedience was rendered to God not by sinners, but by Jesus' righteous life. The penalty for sin was paid, not symbolically through animal sacrifice, but truly by the death of God's Son. And life was brought back to the spiritually dead through the resurrection of Jesus. This was a covenant of grace where the only condition to enter into it is faith in Jesus, and there is no way to break the covenant once entered. In Jesus, salvation had arrived.

Chapter 2

———

THE LIFE OF CHRIST

The life of Jesus Christ is one of substitution and sacrifice, love and compassion. He is a true Savior who in His life fulfilled all righteousness and became our righteousness. His life saves us and shows us the way of godliness.

JESUS OUR EXAMPLE

Most people think of Jesus as a good example: a good man, a good teacher. And that He is! While Jesus is more than an example to follow, He is the perfect example of what humanity and obedience to God look like.

Jesus not only commands us to be servants of one another, but also shows us what humble service looks like. After washing the feet of His disciples, a task typically reserved for servants and those of low social standing,

Jesus said,

> *Do you understand what I have done to you? You*
> *call me Teacher and Lord, and you are right, for so*
> *I am. If I then, your Lord and Teacher, have washed*
> *your feet, you also ought to wash one another's*
> *feet. For I have given you an example, that you also*
> *should do just as I have done to you.*
>
> (JOHN 13:12-15)

When we are instructed in holy living, we are told to emulate Jesus:

> *Put on then, as God's chosen ones, holy and*
> *beloved, compassionate hearts, kindness, humility,*
> *meekness, and patience, bearing with one another*
> *and, if one has a complaint against another, forgiv-*
> *ing each other; as the Lord has forgiven you, so you*
> *also must forgive.*
>
> (COL. 3:12-13)

Further, "Therefore be imitators of God, as beloved children. And walk in love, as Christ loved us and gave himself up for us, a fragrant offering and sacrifice to God" (Eph. 5:1–2).

To be imitators of Jesus does not make us counterfeit. Rather, it shows that we are authentic disciples (Matt. 16:24; John 15:8), because Jesus modeled the perfect life of justice, mercy, and walking with God (see Mic.

6:8). In Jesus, we see what love for others and submission to the will of God looks like. We learn from Jesus, but this learning would be meaningless without the primary work of Jesus' life.

JESUS OUR SUBSTITUTE

Had Jesus only left us an example to follow, He would have done nothing more than reiterate the law of God. His example says, "Do this." But looking back over biblical history, we see time and again that we ignore and defy God's commands. We have not done His will, but rather our own. All of us have sinned and fall short of God's standard of perfection, missing the goal of glorifying our Creator (Rom. 3:23). There is no exception; none is righteous (Rom. 3:10–18).

Part of the good news of the gospel is that Jesus' exemplary life was also one of substitution. He took the place of sinners to fulfill their responsibilities before the face of God. In every area that we have failed to keep God's commands, Jesus succeeded. In our responsibility to love our neighbors, pray in all things, serve others, forgive those who hurt us, and obey the commands of God, Jesus never failed.

JESUS OUR LAW KEEPER

The "law" of God can have different meanings in different parts of the Bible. The law often means the commands of God, but it also refers to Scripture as a whole. When we consider Jesus as "law keeper," therefore, we should think of the law as the revealed will of God, His standard of righteousness, His commands. Jesus explains that the whole of the law is summarized in loving God and loving our neighbors, which is a breakdown of the Ten Commandments (Matt. 22:34–40). Throughout the Old Testament and the New, all that God calls us to do is an act of love toward Him or others.

God gives us law for three basic reasons. His law shows us what is good, what is wrong, and what is needed.[1] First, God's commands show us what is good—namely, by showing us His ways. The will of God is good, for it comes from the very heart of God. It is good because its source is good. His law is not a list of arbitrary commands designed to make us jump through meaningless hoops. They reflect God's character and work for the good of humanity.

Second, God's law shows us what is wrong. If God's ways are good and we find that we cannot keep those laws, then we should be able to see that we are the problem. This reveals that we are lawbreakers by nature. We know ourselves well enough to see that wherever God has commanded us to obey, we are pulled in the other direction. God says, "Do not covet," yet our hearts yearn for what others have. God says, "Forgive those who sin against you," yet we want to take vengeance against them.

Third, God's law shows us what we need. As lawbreakers, we face God's judgment. The law condemns not only our actions, but us as well. In declaring us guilty, God's law shows us that we need mercy, forgiveness, and righteousness. Apart from the law, we would not know how lost we are and how needy we are of God's saving grace (Rom. 7:7).

Jesus submitted perfectly to the will of God in every area of life. Though He clashed with the religious elites of His day over the proper interpretation and use of the law, Jesus said that He did not come to destroy the law, but to fulfill it (Matt. 5:17).

JESUS OUR RIGHTEOUSNESS

As sinful men and women, we need more than forgiveness. We need righteousness. The life of Jesus was one of perfect submission to God the Father and perfect obedience to the law. Jesus did these things because of who He is by nature. The Son of God could do nothing other than live righteously because He is righteous. His righteous life as our substitute is what allows us to be made righteous. Paul explains,

Indeed, I count everything as loss because of the surpassing worth of knowing Christ Jesus my Lord. For his sake I have suffered the loss of all things and count them as rubbish, in order that I may gain Christ and be found in him, not having a righteousness of my own that comes from the law, but that which comes through faith in Christ, the righteousness from God that depends on faith.

(PHIL. 3:8–9)

Paul understood that he was created to be righteous, but also that was not what he was made to be. There was no hope of him working up a kind of righteousness derived from obeying the law. Our sin runs too deep and our love too shallow. But because Jesus Christ, the Son of God, fulfilled all righteousness and lived on our behalf, we can be made righteous. And that is the reason why we can follow His example. Yet there is more to the story.

—

Chapter 3

THE DEATH AND RESURRECTION OF CHRIST

D̶eath is God's curse on sinful humanity. Death is not good, yet Christians often refer to the death of Jesus as "good." How can the death of a righteous person at the hands of wicked men be good?

OUR SUBSTITUTION

The death of Christ was horrific. Yet, God was working behind the scenes to make this act of unrighteous violence something redemptive. What makes the death of Jesus good is that it was a willing, substitutionary sacrifice for sinners.

From the very beginning, God's plan was for the Son to die. Peter explains,

> *Men of Israel, hear these words: Jesus of Nazareth,*
> *a man attested to you by God with mighty works*
> *and wonders and signs that God did through him*
> *in your midst, as you yourselves know—this Jesus,*
> *delivered up according to the definite plan and*
> *foreknowledge of God, you crucified and killed by*
> *the hands of lawless men.*

(ACTS 2:22–23)

Evil men murdered Jesus. They were not coerced to do so, and yet all of it was part of the plan of God. For salvation to come to the world, a Savior needed to die.

The Jewish Scriptures, the Old Testament, promised Christ's birth, His miracles, and His message. But all of this led up to the moment of His crucifixion, which Scripture also foretold. His betrayal did not catch Him off guard, and His crucifixion was no surprise to Him, though it was to nearly everyone else. Jesus came into the world to save sinners and take away their sin.

Not only was Jesus' death planned, but He was also ready and willing to lay down His life. No one forced Him to do it. Though a fearful and agonizing path, the journey to the cross was what Jesus came to walk.

The death of Christ was necessary, for it was the only means by which One could pay for the sins of many. Just as He was our substitute in His life, so He was in His death. He lived in our stead so we could be counted righteous, and He died on our behalf so we would be forgiven. In taking our place on the cross, Jesus received the just punishment for the sins that we all deserved. The righteous willingly suffered for the unrighteous so we could be made righteous. In this sense, we can say that Jesus died *for us*, to save us. But there is another sense in which we can say that Jesus died *for God*.

OUR SATISFACTION

God is both forgiving and just. This means that He does not forgive sins by waiving their punishment. He cannot simply overlook our corruption. Our transgression and rebellion against God must be punished. This is why Jesus died on the cross. He died to satisfy God's wrath against us. The word that the apostle John uses to explain God's love for us on the cross is *propitiation* (1 John 2:2). The word essentially means "to satisfy." But more specifically, propitiation is the satisfaction of God's wrath against our sin through the death of Jesus Christ (see also Rom. 3:25; Heb. 2:17). Thus, Jesus' death on the cross is the clearest expression of God's justice, because in it He was punishing sin.

Yet Jesus' death is also the clearest expression of God's love for us, and that makes Jesus' death good. Many Christians are assured of God's love through His gentle actions and generous providences. Many believe the proof of God's love can be found in the blessings He gives us in this life. Prayer answered in the way we desire or provision in a time of need might make us feel that God cares for us. Beautiful sunsets, delicious food, a happy family, and a successful career can lead us to believe that God loves us. While these certainly testify to God's love and goodness, we must ask: does God not love those whose lives are characterized by loss, affliction, sorrow, and need?

God's benevolence is seen in the many ways that He provides for both the righteous and the unrighteous (Matt. 5:45), but we cannot look to our circumstances for assurance of God's love. Not only would that lead us to believe that God loves some more than others, and perhaps the wicked more than the righteous, but it also undermines faith.

When we assure ourselves of God's love through what He provides for us, we will then question His love when our needs go unmet. God might appear temperamental, unfair, or uninvolved if we allowed our changing circumstances to be the grid through which we see God's love.

If we cannot base our understanding of God's love for us on our circumstances, what do we base it on?

The apostle John declares, "In this the love of God was made manifest among us, that God sent his only Son into the world, so that we might live through him" (1 John 4:9).

The love of God was manifested, and presented publicly, in the sending of His Son, Jesus Christ. When it comes to the "sending" of the Son of God, this does not merely mean His appearance on earth, but everything from His incarnation to His crucifixion and resurrection (Rom. 8:1, 3; Gal. 4:4–5; 1 John 4:10). God's love is ultimately seen in what He did for us nearly two thousand years ago. And what did God do in sending Jesus? He sent a substitute who would accomplish the righteousness required of us and atone for the sins we have committed.

How do we know God loves us? Because Jesus died for us. Through His sacrifice, sin is paid for and God's wrath against us has been satisfied. When we wonder what God thinks of us as His people, when we are in doubt of God's affection for us, all we need to do is look back. God's love cannot be measured by the worldly gifts received today, but by God's ultimate gift given two thousand years ago in His Son. God's love is seen best not in His providence in our lives, but in the divine propitiation Jesus made for our sins.

OUR VICTORY

The death of Jesus is the message of the church. We preach Christ crucified (1 Cor. 1:23). The church is called to bear witness to Jesus, and the central act in His earthly life was His death.

But the death of Jesus would be nothing more than the death of another prophet or preacher if it were not for His resurrection from the grave. Jesus' resurrection demonstrates His authority and victory over death. It was also a promise to us.

The Spirit that raised Jesus from the dead will also give life to our mortal bodies by raising us from the dead, reuniting soul and body and leading us into eternal paradise. The resurrection of Jesus gives us hope that we, too, will be resurrected. But there's another promise given to us in the resurrection of Jesus, the promise of power to live a godly life.

The Spirit that raised Jesus from the dead is the same Spirit that made us alive when we were spiritually dead. The Holy Spirit caused us to be born again and now dwells in us, teaches us, leads us, fills us, and sanctifies us.

There is no good news for sinners if Jesus did not live a perfect life on our behalf. Nor is there good news for us if He did not die on the cross for sins. Nor is there any good news if Jesus did not also rise from the dead. All this is the gospel. It is history, and it is foundation for our doctrine.

the DOCTRINE OF THE GOSPEL

The gospel is the life, death, and resurrection of Jesus Christ by which He fulfilled God's law, atoned for sin, and gives life to all who believe. The Christian's identity and eternity is wrapped up in what Jesus has done on our behalf. This gospel that we have received grants us every spiritual blessing, some of which need to be unpacked and applied in order to fully understand and experience the grace we have in Jesus. There are many gospel doctrines that are found in Jesus, and in these next six chapters we will explore some of the most important.

Chapter 4

JUSTIFICATION

Believers treasure many doctrines central to the Christian faith, but there is none more precious to the church than the doctrine of justification. This is the heart of our theological body, giving life to the whole. Were we to remove this doctrine from our theology, we would never properly understand what it means to be reconciled to God.

JUST CONDEMNATION

Before we can understand and delight in the doctrine of justification, however, we must first comprehend and mourn the reality of our deserved condemnation, a reality we touched upon earlier. All of us are sinners and are justly condemned for what we have done in thought, word, and deed. The apostle Paul, quoting the Old Testament, paints a dark yet entirely realistic picture of our condition:

None is righteous, no, not one;
  no one understands;
  no one seeks for God.
All have turned aside; together they have
    become worthless;
  no one does good,
  not even one.
Their throat is an open grave;
  they use their tongues to deceive.
The venom of asps is under their lips.
  Their mouth is full of curses and bitterness.
Their feet are swift to shed blood;
  in their paths are ruin and misery,
and the way of peace they have not known.
  There is no fear of God before their eyes.
(ROM. 3:10–18)

Believing that one is a sinner is a step in the right direction, but it is not enough. We must see not only that we have broken God's law, gone our own way, and worshiped false gods, but also that our sin is worthy of God's wrath. We are sinners by nature and deserve divine punishment. Not until one hears the threat of God's judgment and admits, "That is what I deserve," will one understand justification.

Our just condemnation is the fair verdict of our guilt before God and the perfect sentencing for our crimes.

We have sinned and deserve hell (Rom. 2:1–29; 6:23).

MERCIFUL JUSTIFICATION

Justification is made possible only by the Son of God, our substitute. The Righteous One stands in our place, receiving the judgment we deserve; and we stand in Him, having been forgiven and reconciled to God. Paul explains,

> *For our sake he made him to be sin who knew no sin, so that in him we might become the righteousness of God.*
>
> (2 COR. 5:21)

Justification consists of two acts of kindness from God: the forgiveness of sin and the imputation of Christ's righteousness. We will consider forgiveness in more detail in the next chapter, but for now we need to understand that God can forgive our sins only if those very sins are atoned for. On the cross, Jesus offered Himself as the sacrifice, the atonement for our sins. This is how we are forgiven.

But forgiveness alone is not enough. Even if all our sins are taken away, we still lack the righteousness God demands of us. We still do not measure up to God's standards. Our status before God needs to change.

The moment a person believes in Jesus as Lord and

Savior, he or she is declared to be holy. This holiness is not something that is seen or felt. It is not the perfection of our lives, but the "imputation" of Jesus' righteousness to us. To impute righteousness is not to infuse it into our souls, but to declare us to be righteous by virtue of our union with Jesus. His righteousness is given to us as a gift so that we are cleansed of all guilt and made perfect in God's sight.

The apostle Paul had no confidence in his own righteousness, but was confident before the face of God on account of Christ's righteousness credited to him:

> *Indeed, I count everything as loss because of the surpassing worth of knowing Christ Jesus my Lord. For his sake I have suffered the loss of all things and count them as rubbish, in order that I may gain Christ and be found in him, not having a righteousness of my own that comes from the law, but that which comes through faith in Christ, the righteousness from God that depends on faith.*
>
> (PHIL. 3:8–9)

To be justified is to be pardoned, purified, and perfected in the sight of God through the death of Jesus on our behalf. This is the foundation of our peace with God. This is the doctrine that frees the conscience to rejoice, worship, and approach God without fear of judgment. Though we have sinned, do sin, and will continue to sin in this life, we can rejoice that God has forgiven it all. We can worship and obey God, and though such acts are imperfect, they are considered perfect by God because of what Christ has done for us.

> *Therefore, since we have been justified by faith, we have peace with God through our Lord Jesus Christ. Through him we have also obtained access by faith into this grace in which we stand, and we rejoice in hope of the glory of God.*

(ROM. 5:1–2)

Chapter 5

—

FORGIVENESS

*F*orgiveness of sin is the most critical need of humanity. Above happiness, health, and even life is our need to be forgiven by God, against whom we have sinned.

Though God is just and good in condemning sin and judging sinners, He is also merciful and forgiving. He is a God who punishes sin and forgives sin. This is how God describes Himself to Moses in the book of Exodus:

> *The LORD, the LORD, a God merciful and gracious, slow to anger, and abounding in steadfast love and faithfulness, keeping steadfast love for thousands, forgiving iniquity and transgression and sin, but who will by no means clear the guilty, visiting the iniquity of the fathers on the children and the children's children, to the third and the fourth generation.*
>
> (34:6–7)

Because God is holy, He cannot overlook sin or pretend that it does not exist. His just nature demands that crimes be punished and that righteousness reign. To not respond to sin justly would require God to stop being God. Yet, while He says He will and must punish sin, God also declares that He is merciful, gracious, slow to anger, abounding in love, and forgiving.

THE GROUNDS FOR FORGIVENESS

To forgive someone is to extend mercy to them by not feeling anger toward them or continuing to hold their offense against them. It is a kind of pardoning of the guilty. As Christians, our forgiveness of others is rooted in God's forgiveness of us (Eph. 4:32).

When God forgives sinners, He no longer counts their sins against them. Instead, He pardons them of their crimes, removes their guilt, and restores or establishes a positive relationship with them (Eph. 1:7; Rom. 8:1). Forgiveness is the heart of the good news that Christians preach and is the dominant message preached throughout the book of Acts (Acts 2:38; 5:31; 10:43; 13:38; 26:18). This forgiveness of sins is what we have received, what we confess, and what we preach as the church.

Too many churches have too many competing messages in their own "outreach." True, we need prophetic voices condemning injustice and apologetics to combat false doctrines. But the central message the church is called to hold out before the world is that forgiveness of sins and reconciliation with God is offered in Jesus Christ and no one else.

But, as we discussed earlier, forgiveness cannot be offered at the expense of justice. Our just God must punish sin while extending the grace of forgiveness. How can God do both? Like all gospel promises, the answer is found in Jesus Christ.

> For there is no distinction: for all have sinned and fall short of the glory of God, and are justified by his grace as a gift, through the redemption that is in Christ Jesus, whom God put forward as a propitiation by his blood, to be received by faith. This was to show God's righteousness, because in his divine forbearance he had passed over former sins. It was to show his righteousness at the present time, so that he might be just and the justifier of the one who has faith in Jesus.
>
> (ROM. 3:22–26)

All of humanity is guilty. We deserve condemnation and need forgiveness. We understand that forgiveness is undeserved kindness, but such kindness comes at a price. Justice is served at the great cost of the life of God's Son.

The only way God can forgive the guilty is if another takes the place and punishment of the guilty. That substitute has to be able to bear all the guilt of the sinner in order to satisfy the just wrath of God. Jesus is the only substitute capable of such work. As the eternal Son of God who is also fully human, He alone was able to be the substitute for not only one guilty sinner, but for all sinners who believe in Him. He received all of God's judgment for the guilty, becoming a propitiation for our sins. The full and exact payment of God's justice was by the Savior, allowing God both to punish sin in Jesus and forgive sinners on account of what He has done.

While the gift of forgiveness was costly for Jesus, it is free for sinners and received by faith alone. The moment a sinner believes, they are forever forgiven, pardoned, and reconciled to God.

THE FRUIT OF FORGIVENESS

The grace of forgiveness absolves the guilty and cleanses the filthy. But as one understands and meditates on this truth it becomes transformative by producing in him humility, gratitude, joy, and boasting.

Humility is a condition of the heart that recognizes the greatness of God and the frailty of human beings. Being humble does not mean that one considers themselves nothing. Rather, it means one knows the truth about their condition: they are needy, broken creatures in need of God's mercy.

Gratitude is the natural result of our forgiveness, for God has done for us what we could never do ourselves. The burden of guilt and the fear of hell have been removed, and we are left with an overwhelming sense of thankfulness for the mercy we have received. Gratitude is a freedom that comes with the meeting of a great need and moves us to cherish what we have received without taking it for granted.

Joy follows forgiveness, as the reality of salvation grants an assurance that nothing can now separate the forgiven sinner from the Forgiver. We experience a deep and abiding delight in the God who saves.

While humility and gratitude keep one from boasting in themselves, joy moves the forgiven to boast in the Lord Jesus. He alone saves. That becomes the theme and message of the pardoned.

All of this in turn leads to the practice of forgiveness. As those who have been forgiven of sins far greater than any committed against us, we are moved to forgive others, even at great cost to ourselves. When we join a local church, we sign up to be sinned against. The local church is a family, and like all families, people will eventually hurt one another. But as people who have experienced the forgiving grace of the Lord, we stand ready to forgive those who sin against us and we seek forgiveness when we sin against a brother or sister.

Chapter 6

FAITH AND REPENTANCE

If the heart of the church is the gospel of grace, then the heart of a believer is one of faith and repentance. Faith and repentance are two sides of the same coin we call "conversion."

Every believer was at one time not a believer. They were unbelievers and unforgiven before they trusted in Jesus. The transition from unbeliever to believer can be experienced as a clear and immediate moment of transformation, while for others their experience is more subtle. The timing and circumstances of one's conversion differ from person to person, but every conversion consists of faith and repentance. Some are converted so early in their lives that they cannot recall a time when they were not converted. Others are converted dramatically at a later age and in such a manner that the event is sealed in their heart forever. And then there are those who remember the days before their conversion, and that they are now believers, but cannot pinpoint the precise moment. Regardless of the manner in which their conversion happens, all Christians are converted in a moment when faith and repentance are present.

FAITH

Faith is often thought of as a leap into the unknown, a blind acceptance of a wish not really based on anything. But Christian faith is not wishing. It is dependence on Christ and His promises and truths revealed in Scripture. Faith is based on what God has said in the light, not a trust fall into the dark. Faith is best understood as being made up of three parts: knowledge, assent, and trust.

Saving faith in Jesus Christ requires knowledge of facts. We cannot believe in Jesus unless we know who He is, what He did, and what it all means. Jesus' righteous life, His sacrificial death, and His resurrection from the grave saves sinners from sin, death, and hell. Unless we know this, true faith is impossible.

But knowledge alone is not yet faith. Many know the truth but do not yet believe it. Knowledge must be accompanied by assent. Assent is agreement with the facts, an acknowledgement that they are true. Some consider themselves to be Christian because they assent to the truth. But even then this is not faith. Many people, and even demons (James 2:19), know the facts and agree that they are indeed true.

Think for a moment of a stool. If you walk up to a three-legged seat, you know what it is—something to sit on. You can see how it is made and know what its purpose is. This is knowledge. You can examine it closely and conclude that if you were to sit on it, it would bear all your weight. Agreeing that it could hold you is assent. But this is not yet faith. Faith happens when you sit on the stool and rest. Such resting is the essence of trust.

Trust, the final ingredient of faith, knows the facts, agrees with the facts, and then moves a person to fully rely on the mercy of God in Christ. To truly believe requires more than a religious head-nod to the promises; it includes receiving and resting upon them. Faith always requires repentance.

REPENTANCE

Most of us have a general understanding of repentance: to turn away from sin. In his *Brief Catechism of Bible Doctrine*, James P. Boyce explains, "Repentance is sorrow for sin, accompanied by a determination, with the help of God, to sin no more."[1]

We cannot turn away from sin completely, not in this lifetime. But faith empowers us to endeavor to forsake sin and walk in righteousness. This, if it will be experienced in any measure, will happen only with divine assistance.

Accompanying such turning is a *godly* sorrow. Not a sorrow for the pain sin has caused us. Not a regret that one has been caught in sin. But a sorrow that is rooted in offending our good and holy God. As Paul writes in 2 Corinthians 7:10, "For godly grief produces a repentance that leads to salvation without regret, whereas worldly grief produces death."

The 1689 Baptist Confession explains repentance as

an evangelical grace, whereby a person, being by the Holy Spirit made sensible of the manifold evils of his sin, does, by faith in Christ, humble himself for it with godly sorrow, detestation of it, and self-abhorrence, praying for pardon and strength of grace, with a purpose and endeavor, by supplies of the Spirit, to walk before God unto all well-pleasing in all things.[2]

Repentant people see their sin, hate their sin, and prayerfully seek to reject their sin and walk with God.

While some of our sins are obvious to us, we comfortably ignore others. We all must prayerfully ask the Holy Spirit to lead us in repentance as we examine our lives in light of the Word and seek to lay aside the sin that so easily entangles us (Heb. 12:1). Repentance includes knowing how to respond practically to these specific sins by replacing them with godly practices.

Repentance is not self-powered moral reformation,

but a spiritual transformation that is accomplished by the work of Jesus Christ. In all our repentance from sin, we must look to Jesus as our only hope for rest from sin, encouragement in growth, and power to live for God. To rest in, be encouraged by, and find power in the gospel, we must prayerfully dwell on the person and work of Jesus. To do this we need robust theology that is continually exercised by faith.

While faith and repentance mark the beginning of the Christian life, they continue on throughout the whole of it as well. An infant comes from her mother's womb drawing her first breath, but she must continue to breathe in order to live. Faith and repentance are like spiritual breathing. We continually breathe in faith and exhale in repentance.

Chapter 7

—

RECONCILIATION

𝔚e cannot fully appreciate the gospel if we fail to understand the nature of our reconciliation to God. Our reconciliation is not merely the patching back together of a fractured relationship, or the smoothing over of hurt feelings. In reconciling sinners to Himself, God turns enemies into friends.

ENEMIES OF GOD

Before conversion, we are not simply unfamiliar with God; we are by nature His enemies (Rom. 5:10). We are not naturally children of God, but rather are "children of wrath," as Paul explains:

> And you were dead in the trespasses and sins in
> which you once walked, following the course of this
> world, following the prince of the power of the air,
> the spirit that is now at work in the sons of dis-
> obedience—among whom we all once lived in the

passions of our flesh, carrying out the desires of the
body and the mind, and were by nature children of
wrath, like the rest of mankind.

(EPH. 2:1–3)

Regardless of their moral standing among other men and women, every human being in their natural condition is hostile and inimical toward God. We follow the devil and the sinful inclinations of our hearts. We are corrupted and unbelieving, and to us nothing is pure; both our minds and consciences are defiled (Titus 1:15). And yet, in our salvation we are made children of God.

CHILDREN OF GOD

God not only forgives us, but also reconciles us to Himself. Former enemies of God become His children. In this dramatic change, we begin to see the depths of God's love for sinners.

But to all who did receive him, who believed in his
name, he gave the right to become children of God,
who were born, not of blood nor of the will of the
flesh nor of the will of man, but of God.

(JOHN 1:12–13).

Our salvation is not a matter of orphans being adopted by God. We are rebels who are redeemed to be a part of God's family (Gal. 4:5).

Yet our reconciliation goes even deeper, for sinners are not only adopted as God's children, but also are made friends of God (John 15:15; James 2:23). Friends dwell in peace, partner in mission, and maintain intimacy. We are bound to God through Jesus Christ as both children and friends. This act of divine reconciliation brands us as reconcilers with a ministry of reconciliation (Rom. 5:11; 2 Cor. 5:18).

THE MINISTRY OF RECONCILIATION

The church of Jesus Christ is not only a reconciled community. It is also a reconciling community. We have peace with God and each other and we are now privileged to hold out the hope of reconciliation to the world:

> *Therefore, if anyone is in Christ, he is a new creation. The old has passed away; behold, the new has come. All this is from God, who through Christ reconciled us to himself and gave us the ministry of reconciliation; that is, in Christ God was reconciling the world to himself, not counting their trespasses against them, and entrusting to us the message of reconciliation. Therefore, we are ambassadors for Christ, God making his appeal through us. We implore you on behalf of Christ, be reconciled to God.*

(2 COR. 5:17–20)

Our experience of God's reconciling grace has made us reconcilers in the name of Jesus. We are ambassadors, representatives of Jesus and the gospel, who urge others to be reconciled to God. We preach Christ crucified and the offer of a new identity and a new relationship with God.

Our experience of reconciliation cannot end with us, but must be extended to everyone we encounter so they, too, might come to know the riches of God's grace. His grace is available to all, offered to all; and to all who receive it, they become the children of God.

___

Chapter 8

SANCTIFICATION

The gospel is the good news of salvation in Jesus Christ. While we tend to focus on the doctrine of justification, the heart of the gospel, we must not lose sight of the doctrine of sanctification, the life of the gospel. Paul writes,

> *But we ought always to give thanks to God for you, brothers beloved by the Lord, because God chose you as the firstfruits to be saved, through sanctification by the Spirit and belief in the truth.*
>
> (2 THESS. 2:13)

God does not just forgive sinners; He transforms them. He progressively and continually restores His image in us, which was defaced by sin, by conforming us to the image of Christ. This is not a mere change in behavior, but a change in heart that gives spiritual life to our whole person.

Sanctification is the work of God in which we partic-

ipate by His grace. In Paul's benediction in 1 Thessalonians 5:23, we learn that our growth in godliness is the
work of God: "Now may the God of peace himself sanctify you completely, and may your whole spirit and soul
and body be kept blameless at the coming of our Lord
Jesus Christ." The Christian's transformation is holistic.
It includes spirit, soul, and body. This verse shows us
that God changes the whole person—from the inside
out. It is His work in us.

This is why Jesus prays to the Father that He would
sanctify us (John 17:17). More specifically, we see that
it is the Holy Spirit who is at work in us. In showing the
contrast between unbelievers and the people of God,
Paul writes, "And such were some of you. But you were
washed, you were sanctified, you were justified in the
name of the Lord Jesus Christ and by the Spirit of our
God" (1 Cor. 6:11). Christians are no longer who they
once were. God has made us new and is making us new.
We have different identities, different lives.

But God does not do this work in us arbitrarily. He
does it through the ministry of the Word. Jesus prays
that the Father would sanctify us through the truth of
His Word (John 17:17). The Spirit of God uses the
Word of God to progressively transform the people of
God. If we would be sanctified, we must receive the
Word, believe it, and respond to it. No one will be sanc-

tified apart from the work of God or the Word of God.

And while we confess that God's Spirit does the work in us, we actively participate in this process of transformation. We are called to kill sin in our lives, put on righteousness, and actively pursue godliness. In 1 Thessalonians 4:3, we read that God's will for every believer is sanctification. Paul here singles out abstinence from sexual immorality, for abstaining from evil is one of the ways in which we pursue sanctification. Peter likewise tells us to "put away all malice and all deceit and hypocrisy and envy and all slander" (1 Peter 2:1). This is the "negative" aspect of sanctification—putting to death sin in our lives. Yet Peter adds a "positive" command: "Like newborn infants, long for the pure spiritual milk, that by it you may grow up into salvation—if indeed you have tasted that the Lord is good" (1 Peter 2:2–3).

Putting sin to death and pursuing righteousness is what sanctification looks like in the life of a believer. We believe the gospel and obey the gospel. We begin to live different lives because we have been made different by the power of God. The power that makes us new creatures in Jesus Christ is the same power that moves us to pursue godliness. Peter explains,

> *His divine power has granted to us all things that*
> *pertain to life and godliness, through the knowledge*
> *of him who called us to his own glory and excel-*

lence, by which he has granted to us his precious and very great promises, so that through them you may become partakers of the divine nature, having escaped from the corruption that is in the world because of sinful desire. For this very reason, make every effort to supplement your faith with virtue, and virtue with knowledge, and knowledge with self-control, and self-control with steadfastness, and steadfastness with godliness, and godliness with brotherly affection, and brotherly affection with love. For if these qualities are yours and are increasing, they keep you from being ineffective or unfruitful in the knowledge of our Lord Jesus Christ.

(2 PETER 1:3–8)

God sanctifies us and calls us to be active in the process. As the Spirit produced His fruit in us, we bear the responsibility to be a people of love, joy, peace, patience, kindness, faithfulness, gentleness, and self-control.

Chapter 9

GOOD WORKS

When people think of "good works," they often think of good deeds, acts of kindness, and various kinds of religious service. These deeds may contain aspects of good works, but there is much more to what the Bible means when it teaches us about good works.

Many Christians have become confused about works as a theological and practical issue. After all, we are not saved by our works, but by God's grace alone. So how should we think about works? What is their role in the Christian life?

In general, "works" are acts of obedience to the revealed will of God. But more specifically, the Bible talks about two kinds of works: dead works and good works.

DEAD WORKS

There is a kind of works that do not please God, and, in fact, are a form of sin. They look good on the outside, but inwardly they are rotten and offensive to God. These are called "dead works."

> *Therefore let us leave the elementary doctrine of Christ and go on to maturity, not laying again a foundation of repentance from dead works and of faith toward God.*
>
> (HEB. 6:1)

Dead works are those acts of obedience that do not stem from faith in Jesus Christ and a love for God. They are not the response of a joyful and grateful heart that has experienced saving grace. Instead, these works are motivated by pride, ambition, or vanity and are aimed at earning God's favor. This is one of the most dangerous, and common, religious traps into which people fall. The hope is that if we can be good enough and work hard enough, then God will accept us or reward us. This is self-righteousness. God's favor cannot be bought. Even if it could, we could not afford it. We have no spiritual currency. Even if our works could merit something, they would not cleanse us from the sins we have committed.

When God calls us to repent of our sins, we are also called to repent of our dead works of self-righteousness. Until we leave behind these works, we cannot live by faith, which produces a different kind of works that please God (Heb. 6:1). The fundamental problem with dead works is that they stem from an unbelieving heart. For "without faith it is impossible to please him" (Heb. 11:6).

The gospel proclaims the only means by which we can be forgiven and cleansed from this particular sin: "the blood of Christ, who through the eternal Spirit offered himself without blemish to God, [will] purify our conscience from dead works to serve the living God" (Heb. 9:14). The death of Jesus Christ saves and cleanses self-righteous sinners from their own dead works, which have polluted their souls. His blood changes us and frees us to serve the Lord by way of good works.

GOOD WORKS

Dead works are acts of obedience that do not stem from faith and are designed to bring glory to us. They do not please God. Good works, on the other hand, are acts of obedience that stem from faith and are aimed at God's glory (see Matt. 5:16). God delights in such works.

God chose us before the foundation of the world so that we would be holy and blameless before Him (Eph. 1:4). Jesus died for us so that we would be a people purified and zealous for good works (Titus 2:14). When we were born again by the power of God, we were recreated to walk in the good works that God has prepared before us (Eph. 2:10).

While we have been saved to walk in good works, every Christian comes to see that even our best acts of obedience to the Lord remain imperfect and are marked by sin (see Rom. 7:7–25). Many Christians become frustrated when they find that, even after transformation, their love, faith, and obedience are still tainted by corruption. Yet God still delights in our imperfect obedience and good works. Tabitha was a woman described in Scripture as being full of good works (Acts 9:36), and we are told that we should and can spur one another on toward good works (Heb. 10:24). How can God approve of and delight in our good works when they still tainted by sin? How can anyone be said to be "filled with good works" when sin remains in them as well?

There are three reasons our good, though imperfect, works are considered good and acceptable before God. First, God accepts our good works because Jesus, in His earthly life, has obeyed the Father perfectly on our behalf. Jesus' righteousness has been credited to us making us and our works perfect in God's eyes.

Second, God accepts our good works because they originate from our faith in Jesus Christ. These are not the works of unbelievers who are working for themselves, but rather are the efforts of God's children, who work to honor their Father in heaven.

Third, God delights in our good works because such works are His own work in us. Paul writes,

> *Therefore, my beloved, as you have always obeyed,*
> *so now, not only as in my presence but much more*
> *in my absence, work out your own salvation with*
> *fear and trembling, for it is God who works in you,*
> *both to will and to work for his good pleasure.*

(PHIL. 2:12–13)

Paul tells us that we are responsible to live out the implications of our salvation, but that our desires, impulses, and actions are evidence of God working in us for His good pleasure.

God delights in the good works of His people because they themselves are the work of God, stem from faith, and are made acceptable by Jesus Christ.

The good works of the Christian faith do not merely make up select parts of the Christian life. Our works are not just prayer, fasting, and Bible study. The good works of the Christian life make up the whole. It includes everything from worship on the Lord's Day to washing dishes after dinner, for all of life is an ongoing response to the God who made us and saved us. We work, in our employment and in areas of personal responsibility, not for others or for ourselves, but for the Lord (Col. 3:23–24). We seek God's glory in all we do and present ourselves as living sacrifices to the God of mercies.

The gospel is, in part, obedience and good works. Not our good works, but Jesus' good works on our behalf. And that gospel gift is what produces in us the good works of faith.

PART 3

the GOD OF THE GOSPEL

Because the gospel is what God has done for us in His Son, Jesus Christ, it is important for us to see exactly what God has done and does in us today. If the gospel truly is all of grace, then it is all of God and not of ourselves.

What does God do to save someone? How involved is He in our coming to Jesus? Is He waiting for us to figure things out, dropping clues along the way in hopes that we will come to our senses and believe the gospel we hear preached by others? Or must He do more? To appreciate and marvel at the gospel, we must look more closely at the God of the gospel.

Chapter 10

———

GOD CONDEMNS JUSTLY

The Bible paints a picture of humanity that is simultaneously beautiful and ugly. All people are made in God's image and exist for His glory. As such, we have worth and dignity beyond all other creatures of the world. Yet all of humanity has rebelled in sin, corrupted the image of God within themselves, and fallen short of God's glory (Rom. 3:23).

Many assume that if God exists, they are most likely on good terms with Him. Even if they do not acknowledge God, they reason, they have done no real harm, broken no serious laws. Plus they can always point to people who are worse than they are. But Scripture reveals that we all "like sheep have gone astray; we have turned—every one—to his own way" (Isa. 53:6).

Does our sin really deserve God's wrath? Are the sins we commit in the span of our earthly life worthy of eter-

nal judgment? Are not we better than so many others?
Scripture is clear regarding these questions:

> Therefore you have no excuse, O man, every one
> of you who judges. For in passing judgment on
> another you condemn yourself, because you, the
> judge, practice the very same things. We know that
> the judgment of God rightly falls on those who
> practice such things. Do you suppose, O man—you
> who judge those who practice such things and
> yet do them yourself—that you will escape the
> judgment of God? Or do you presume on the riches
> of his kindness and forbearance and patience, not
> knowing that God's kindness is meant to lead you
> to repentance? But because of your hard and im-
> penitent heart you are storing up wrath for yourself
> on the day of wrath when God's righteous judgment
> will be revealed.
>
> (ROM. 2:1–5)

No one is innocent before God. Even our sense of
moral superiority is the sin of pride that neglects the
evil inside ourselves. Our hearts are hard, resistant
to the things of God and unyielding to His call. With
each passing day that we continue in our sin, our guilt
increases and God's patience will eventually come to
an end. We are sinners, and sin must be condemned.
The entire human race is sinful in every part. There are
no exceptions. Recalling the words that the apostle
Paul quoted from the Old Testament:

None is righteous, no, not one;

no one understands;

no one seeks for God.

All have turned aside; together they have
  become worthless;

no one does good,

not even one.

Their throat is an open grave;

they use their tongues to deceive.

The venom of asps is under their lips.

Their mouth is full of curses and bitterness.

Their feet are swift to shed blood;

in their paths are ruin and misery,

and the way of peace they have not known.

There is no fear of God before their eyes.

(ROM. 3:10–18)

No one does good, no one seeks God, not even one.

This does not mean, however, that all people are devoid of all goodness. Some people behave better than others. Many people are truly virtuous and model lives that others can imitate. Sinners can be kind and compassionate and generous. We can be *civilly* righteous and relatively good before our peers, but before the face of God we are known to be what we truly are—unrighteous. He sees the imperfections in our best deeds and knows the wrong motives driving our actions.

OUR SIN IS HOLISTIC

All Christians believe that men and women were created good by God (see Genesis 1 and 2). But after our fall into sin, our nature was corrupted and we now stand as sinners before God. That we are depraved is agreed upon by all Christians. But to what extent are we depraved? How deeply has our sin corrupted us? Are we weakened by sin? Made sick by it? Or worse?

The sad reality is that our whole being is corrupted. No one part of us is untouched by sin's stain and power. Our thoughts, words, and actions all are sinful. Our hearts and minds are equally corrupt.

We are not only tangled up in sin, but are completely bound by it. We are not spiritually sick, but are spiritually dead. Paul explains,

> *And you were dead in the trespasses and sins in which you once walked, following the course of this world, following the prince of the power of the air, the spirit that is now at work in the sons of disobedience—among whom we all once lived in the passions of our flesh, carrying out the desires of the body and the mind, and were by nature children of wrath, like the rest of mankind.*
>
> (EPH. 2:1–3)

The depth of our depravity renders us spiritually dead. We are defiled and unbelieving, impure in mind and conscience (Titus 1:15). In fact, our sin goes so deep and our hearts are so corrupt that we are incapable of doing anything spiritually good and thus pleasing to God. This includes honoring Christ as Lord and believing in Him as Savior.

OUR WILLS ARE BOUND

This means that we cannot come to Jesus on our own strength. In John's Gospel, we read of Jesus preaching to a large crowd. He earnestly calls them to believe in Him and tells them that if they do they will inherit eternal life. Yet in the midst of their unbelief, He makes a startling statement: "No one can come to me unless the Father who sent me draws him" (John 6:44).

Jesus teaches not only that we are depraved, but that we are *totally* depraved—meaning that every part of who we are is corrupted by sin. This means that even our wills are bound by sin, and to the extent that we cannot even do what He asks us to do—believe—apart from the sovereign work of God. We do not have it in us to come to Jesus. We cannot change who we are. This limitation is not put upon us by God, but was brought upon ourselves by our own rebellion against Him.

Therefore, God is just in condemning all sinners, for even though we all sin somewhat differently and to varying degrees, we are all totally depraved. And that is why we need grace. The church is made of imperfect people, sinners who have received grace, guilty men and women who have been forgiven, rebels who have been restored to God.

—

Chapter 11

GOD SAVES SOVEREIGNLY

If we are so sinful that we cannot come to Jesus for salvation, then how can anyone be saved? The answer is found in one word: grace.

THE GRACE OF GOD'S CHOICE

Salvation is the work of God—at every level. He alone saves sinners. When the disciples begin to understand how impossible salvation is, Jesus reminds them, "With man this is impossible, but with God all things are possible" (Matt. 19:26).

How does God save sinners? Only through the life, death, and resurrection of Jesus. But God's saving work starts long before that, before the creation of heaven and earth. Paul writes,

Blessed be the God and Father of our Lord Jesus
Christ, who has blessed us in Christ with every
spiritual blessing in the heavenly places, even as he
chose us in him before the foundation of the world,
that we should be holy and blameless before him.
In love he predestined us for adoption to himself as
sons through Jesus Christ, according to the purpose
of his will, to the praise of his glorious grace, with
which he has blessed us in the Beloved.

(EPH.1:3-6)

Before time began, God had already chosen to save sinners. This was not a general plan, but a specific plan to save specific people who, together, would form one people made of men and women from every tribe, tongue, and nation. This plan to save is called the doctrine of election.

The doctrine of election teaches us that God chose a great number of individuals to be saved, long before they were created. His choosing was not based on His seeing anything good in them. It was not based on a foreseen faith that they would exercise, for no one can believe apart from the sovereign working of God. Rather, God's choice of some is in accord with the mysterious "purpose of his will." It is mysterious indeed why God choose some and not all. But we can see and trust that He is good nevertheless. For in choosing some, He demonstrates how gracious He is.

This choice of some, and not all, leaves many feeling that God is unfair, that He plays favorites. But this is better than fair. This is grace. Fairness is justice, and justice requires condemnation of sin and sinners. If God were only fair, He would condemn all. But He is gracious and kind, and He chose to save some rather than leave all condemned in their sin. And this number of elect is no small number, but a number as great as the stars in the sky (Gen. 15:5; Gal. 3:29).

Even so, if God chose to save only one person and no more, this would still be grace. It would be an epic demonstration of kindness toward an undeserving soul. But God has gone far beyond this to save a people for His own possession.

Remember, God chose Abram out of all the people of the world to make a covenant with him, promising that a nation and eventually the Savior would come from him. He chose Isaac, not Ishmael. He chose Jacob, not Esau. All of this reflects God's prerogative to choose one over another. In each of these cases, they were chosen not because they were righteous, but were chosen according to God's will.

When we understand that all people deserve death and hell, the salvation of any demonstrates that God is amazingly gracious. In election, God ensures our salvation. He appoints us to eternal life, and in time He works effectively to convert those He has chosen. We have no right to complain about God's choice, for He gives us either what we have chosen for ourselves (this is justice), or what He has chosen to give us in Christ (this is mercy). As Paul says,

> *What shall we say then? Is there injustice on God's part? By no means! For he says to Moses, "I will have mercy on whom I have mercy, and I will have compassion on whom I have compassion." So then it depends not on human will or exertion, but on God, who has mercy.*

(ROM. 9:14–16)

This raises questions for us. If God has already chosen some for salvation, then why do we need to preach the gospel? Does not His electing grace save them?

THE GUARANTEE OF GOD'S CHOICE

God's election of individuals *ensures* their salvation, but does not *accomplish* their salvation. Christ had to die on the cross, and the elect must believe in Him in order to receive eternal life. The elect will respond positively to the gospel when it is preached. God has predestined the end (salvation) and works through means (preaching) to bring that end to pass. He sends the church into the world to preach God's grace. While many will reject this message, the elect will believe through the ministry of the Word and Spirit.

When Paul and Barnabas preached to a large crowd, many denied the truth because by nature we all suppress the truth. But some believed: "And when the Gentiles heard this, they began rejoicing and glorifying the word of the Lord, *and as many as were appointed to eternal life believed*" (Acts 13:48; emphasis added).

God saves sinners. His plan to save began long before the world was made, is experienced in the lives of the elect, and will continue on until glory: "And those whom he predestined he also called, and those whom he called he also justified, and those whom he justified he also glorified" (Rom. 8:30).

THE ENCOURAGEMENT OF GOD'S CHOICE

The doctrine of election is a gospel truth. It is pure grace. And it should move the church to be zealous in evangelism, for we cannot fail so long as we preach. In fact, God's sovereign election guarantees our success. People will believe. Sinners will be converted. God has not sent us out to harvest a field that will produce no fruit. Rather, He sends us out to bring in all whom He has set apart for Himself. God will save sinners. It is His job, and we trust Him.

This mysterious doctrine of election humbles us, for

we know we would never have come to love God if He had not loved us first. We would not choose Him if He had not first chosen us. Humility, awe, and worship are just some of the fruits this doctrine should produce in the heart of faith. It distills the truth that we contribute nothing to our salvation. It is all of grace, and we now stand in that grace.

Chapter 12

—

GOD ATONES EFFECTIVELY

Those God chose for salvation before the foundation of the world must have their sins atoned. Their guilt must be removed; God's wrath must be satisfied. This could happen only through the death of Jesus Christ.

To say that Jesus died for sinners is a beautiful gospel statement. He died for us. He took our place. He was a true substitute. As such, He did not make salvation *possible* for some, but made it *certain* for many.

Jesus came into the world with a mission: to "save his people from their sins" (Matt. 1:21). He was born to die and rise again, and in doing so, to save the sheep of His pasture, those given to Him by the Father, the church.

Just as the old covenant priests prayed and made sacrifices on behalf of Israel, so Jesus prays for and makes atonement for His people. In John 17, we read of Jesus' High Priestly prayer, which He prayed the night before

His sacrificial death of atonement. Early in His prayer, Jesus says to the Father,

> *I have manifested your name to the people whom you gave me out of the world. Yours they were, and you gave them to me, and they have kept your word. Now they know that everything that you have given me is from you. For I have given them the words that you gave me, and they have received them and have come to know in truth that I came from you; and they have believed that you sent me. I am praying for them. I am not praying for the world but for those whom you have given me, for they are yours. All mine are yours, and yours are mine, and I am glorified in them.*

(JOHN 17:6–10)

Jesus has in mind a particular people. He is seeking the good of those the Father gave Him, who received the truth and believed in Him. He is praying for them, and not the rest of the world.

As the Good Shepherd, Jesus says that He lays down His life for His sheep. He knows His sheep, and they know Him and follow Him. He is emphatic that those who do not believe in Him are not His sheep (John 10:26). Jesus died on the cross for His sheep, for the church (Eph. 5:25). His death was sufficient to save everyone, but is only efficient to save the elect, for He had in mind a specific people when He offered Himself for our sins.

The mission of Christ was not to save as many people as possible, but to save a particular people: those the Father had given Him, the elect. Jesus came to save and build a church that would glorify Him. This was the mission He accomplished. The last words of our Savior are telling. Moments before bowing His head and dying on the cross, Jesus said, "It is finished" (John 19:30).

What did Jesus finish? The work of salvation. In living and dying, Jesus did everything that was necessary to meet God's standard of righteousness, satisfy His demand for justice, remove our guilt, and reconcile us to God. There was and is nothing more to do for our salvation. Now that it has been accomplished, we can receive it by faith as a gift from our God and Savior, Jesus Christ.

—

Chapter 13

GOD CALLS
IRRESISTIBLY

Our depravity has made us all unwilling and unable to humble ourselves before Jesus and receive Him as Lord. In our sinful state, we are spiritually dead with hearts of stone that do not work as God originally designed. Our sin has killed our affection for and submission to God. So how is it that anyone is actually converted?

God the Father chose us in Christ before the foundation of the world, God the Son died for us to accomplish our redemption, and God the Holy Spirit works in the hearts of the elect to bring them to faith in Christ.

THE FATHER GIVES

In John 6, Jesus talks about the people the Father had given Him (see also 17:9) That this is a reference to believers as opposed to nonbelievers is clear. This is a distinct group of people characterized by faith. But there is more:

> *I am the bread of life; whoever comes to me shall not hunger, and whoever believes in me shall never thirst. But I said to you that you have seen me and yet do not believe. All that the Father gives me will come to me, and whoever comes to me I will never cast out.*
>
> (JOHN 6:35–37)

Jesus tells His listeners that they must come to Him to be saved. This is another way of explaining that they must believe Him to be the Son of God who takes away sin and depend on Him alone for their redemption. He tells them that if they believe, they will be saved. Jesus draws a line between those who have believed and those who have not, and then says, "All the Father gives to me will come to me."

Jesus identifies those who believe as those the Father has given Him. There is a number of individuals who will believe the gospel, who will be converted. And Jesus says it is those who are presented to Him as a gift from the Father. These are the same people Jesus prays for in John 17: "I am not praying for the world but for those whom you have given me, for they are yours. All mine are yours, and yours are mine, and I am glorified in them" (John 17:9–10).

Those the Father gives to Jesus are then drawn to Jesus by the will of the Father. In the middle of delivering this difficult message to a large crowd, Jesus confronts the unbelievers and says, "No one can come to me unless the Father who sent me draws him. And I will raise him up on the last day" (John 6:44).

Here Jesus explains that one's refusal to trust Him is an issue of nature. To say no one can come to Jesus apart from the will of the Father is to say more than they are unwilling. They are incapable. The only way people come to Jesus is by the sovereign drawing of the Father.

Of those who are drawn to Christ, all are saved. Jesus promises to give eternal life to, and confirm at the resurrection, everyone who is drawn to Him by the Father.

THE SPIRIT MAKES NEW

If we look more closely at what happens when someone is converted, we see they are changed by the Holy Spirit. Apart from this work of the Spirit, no one is converted.

Jesus' words to Nicodemus in John 3 speak to this reality. As the religious man comes to Jesus, asking questions, Jesus tells him that he must be "born again." Confusion ensues. Nicodemus asks, "How can a man be born when he is old? Can he enter a second time into his mother's womb and be born?" (John 3:4). Jesus answered,

> *Truly, truly, I say to you, unless one is born of water*
> *and the Spirit, he cannot enter the kingdom of God.*
> *That which is born of the flesh is flesh, and that*
> *which is born of the Spirit is spirit. Do not marvel*
> *that I said to you, "You must be born again." The*
> *wind blows where it wishes, and you hear its sound,*
> *but you do not know where it comes from or where it*
> *goes. So it is with everyone who is born of the Spirit.*

(JOHN 3:5–8)

Jesus tells Nicodemus that being "born again" is a spiritual birth worked by the Holy Spirit. It cannot be controlled, but its work can be seen. Why is being born again so important? Because only by being born again can we be changed and do what we could not before—believe.

Consider the story of Lydia. In Acts 16, the apostle Paul finds a group of ladies praying, and he preaches the gospel to them. Lydia was converted. Why? Because she was smarter? Because she was more spiritual than the others? No, she trusted in Christ that day because the Father had given her to Jesus. In that particular moment, the Holy Spirit worked in her in such a way that she listened, heard, believed, and was baptized:

> *One who heard us was a woman named Lydia, from*
> *the city of Thyatira, a seller of purple goods, who*
> *was a worshiper of God.* The Lord opened her
> heart to pay attention to what was said by Paul.

(ACTS 16:14; *emphasis added*)

This new birth is called *regeneration*. It is the spiritual change of heart by the power of the Holy Spirit through the ministry of the Word, which makes us spiritually alive and new creations in Christ. The immediate and necessary accompaniment of the new birth, or regeneration, is faith and repentance (2 Thess. 2:13).

Some hear of this and wonder whether we are nothing more than robots. God chooses us, Christ dies for us, and the Holy Spirit converts us. What does our will do in all this?

Regeneration does not mean God makes us something we do not want to be. It means God fixes our hearts so they work properly. And when they do, we love God. Before the fix (the new birth), you do not think, feel, love, or live rightly. But upon being fixed, our dead hearts begin to beat with love for God. As a result of the new birth, we choose Jesus. But we will not and cannot do so apart from God's irresistible grace.

—

Chapter 14

GOD SUSTAINS FAITHFULLY

Just as our coming to Jesus is the result of grace, so too is our continuing with Jesus. Those the Father chose before time began, whom Jesus died for, and whose hearts the Holy Spirit opened will be preserved by God's grace and will persevere until the end of their lives.

No doubt, true believers will struggle with sin. They can and will fail—and sometimes in serious ways. But God will give them the divine help they need so that their faith remains intact and so that they learn repentance.

Jesus says that no one can snatch His disciples out of His hand; they are forever secure (John 10:28–29). Paul tells us that nothing—whether visible or invisible, not distress, or persecution, or famine, or nakedness, or danger, or sword—can separate us from the love of Jesus Christ (Rom. 8:35–39).

Not only is our salvation that secure; our faith is secure

as well. The good work of salvation that God began in us will continue until death or the return of Jesus (Phil. 1:6).

If someone departs fully from the faith, it is evidence that they never truly believed. John touches on this when, speaking of false teachers, he says, "They went out from us, but they were not of us; for if they had been of us, they would have continued with us. But they went out, that it might become plain that they all are not of us" (1 John 2:19).

It is not the presence or prevalence of sin in a person's life that reveals them to be a false convert. Apostasy, the denial of the truth of the gospel once held, is the sure sign. But God's promise to sustain His people is not the guarantee that everyone who claims the name of Jesus will persevere. Many will call themselves Christians, only to later fall away and prove that true faith never took root in their hearts (see Matt. 13:1–23). But those who believe will be preserved by God's grace.

It is important that we understand God's promise to sustain us in the faith is not a promise to keep us from the presence of sin. All believers continue to sin, and sometimes fall deep into transgression, making a mess of their lives and the lives of others. The 1689 Baptist Confession explains well the presence of serious sin in the life of the Christian, its consequences, and God's preserving power:

And though [Christians] may, through the temptation
of Satan and of the world, the prevalency of corruption remaining in them, and the neglect of means
of their preservation, fall into grievous sins, and for
a time continue therein, whereby they incur God's
displeasure and grieve his Holy Spirit, come to have
their graces and comforts impaired, have their hearts
hardened, and their consciences wounded, hurt and
scandalize others, and bring temporal judgments
upon themselves, yet shall they renew their repentance and be preserved through faith in Christ Jesus to
the end.[1]

True converts can backslide. A straight reading of the
Bible shows how often the people of God, even those
who love the Lord and help us as examples, fail. The
world, the flesh, and the devil all work to lead us away
from Jesus Christ, and sometimes they are successful
for a time. We can fall into "grievous sin" and even remain there for a while. And while in that place, we may
suffer circumstantially, but we will certainly suffer spiritually as the graces and comforts of God are "impaired."
But even when we fall, God remains present with us to
lead us back to Himself and to grant us repentance (2
Tim. 2:25).

The confidence of the Christian amidst temptation
and spiritual attack is not *their* faith, but *the* faith. Our
faith, like Peter's, can waver, falter, and fail. Peter denied

Jesus three times shortly after Jesus was arrested. All Christians follow suit in one way or another. Our hope while living in this world that stands against the truth is the faith once for all delivered to the saints—that is, the gospel itself (Jude 3).

Our boldness comes not from how strongly we believe, but how strong the Savior is in whom we believe. He has saved us, will preserve us, and will see that we finish well. To say that God sustains His people means not only that individuals will continue in the faith, but that the church will continue as well. "I will build my church, and the gates of hell shall not prevail against it" (Matt. 16:18).

CONCLUSION

The gospel is the heart of the church. It is not simply one thing we believe, but the defining truth for the Christian and the church. The gospel makes us who we are and the church what it is. In the gospel, we see the glory and grace of God. God's love for sinners, Christ's death for sinners, and the Holy Spirit's conversion of sinners is the outworking of the grace of the gospel.

If the gospel is not the heart of a local church, then something else will be. Something good but less important will become our focus, and we will lose sight of who we are in Jesus, what He calls us to be, and how He calls us to live together as the church. But when the gospel is the heart of the church there is the fruitful life of worship, fellowship, and mission. May the gospel be the defining truth in your life and church always.

NOTES

Part 1: The History of the Gospel

1. "The Apostles' Creed," on *Christian Classics Ethereal Library* website, https://www.ccel.org/creeds/apostles.creed.html (emphasis added).

Chapter 1: The Theme of Scripture

1. Joel Beeke, *Living for God's Glory* (Sanford, FL: Reformation Trust Publishing, 2008), 258.
2. Richard Barcellos, *The Covenant of Works: Its Confessional and Scriptural Basis* (Palmdale, CA: RBAP, 2016), 64.

Chapter 2: The Life of Christ

1. See my book *Note to Self: The Discipline of Preaching to Yourself* (Wheaton, IL: Crossway, 2011).

Chapter 6: Faith and Repentance

1. James P. Boyce, "Brief Catechism of Bible Doctrine," Repentance and Faith, Q1, on *The Reformed Reader* website, http://www.reformedreader.org/ccc/bcbd.htm.

2. "The Baptist Confession of Faith," 15.3, on *The Voice of the Reformation* website, http://www.vor.org/truth/1689/1689bc00.html.

Chapter 14: God Sustains Faithfully
1. "The Baptist Confession of Faith," 17.3, on *The Voice of the Reformation* website, http://www.vor.org/truth/1689/1689bc00.html.

ACKNOWLEDGMENTS

I would like to thank Paul Maxwell for encouraging me to write this book and introducing me to Moody Publishers. Thanks to Drew Dyck, acquisitions editor, and Kevin Emmert, developmental editor, for helping me clarify and better communicate what is on my heart. This book is greatly improved by your efforts.

Thanks to the leadership of Redeemer Fellowship—Jeff Willey, Pat Aldridge, Brian Malcolm, Rob Warford, and Jimmy Fowler—and the entire congregation for showing me what a healthy church looks like in real life.

And thank you to my wife, Jen, and our children, Katherine, Elias, Madeline, and Kilian, for being patient with me during the time it took to write this book.

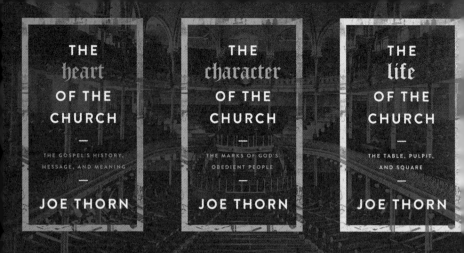

THE *life* | *heart* | *character* OF THE CHURCH

This three-book series is designed for diverse readership. It avoids theological jargon and uses clear terms to keep readers tracking and engaged. Ideal for evangelism and discipleship, each book can be read within an hour and is organized simply for retention. Biblical, balanced, and historically informed, it is useful for Sunday school, one-to-one reading, ministry training, and personal study.

FOR THE
CHURCH

FTC.CO

MOODY
Publishers®

moodypublishers.com

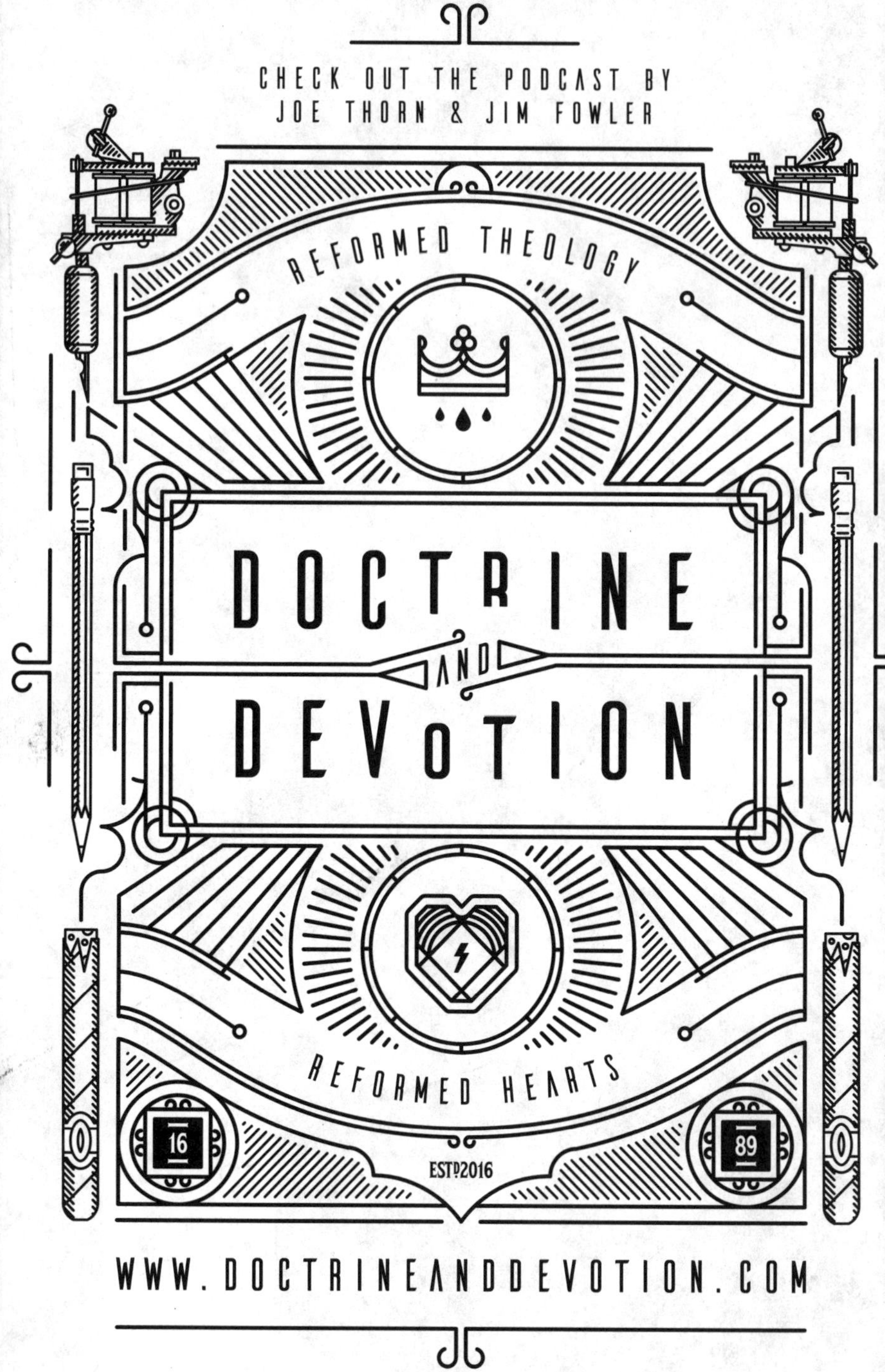